My Running Log Book

Barb Asselin

Asselin Group Online Publisher
R.R. #2, 449 Flat Rapids Road
Arnprior, ON Canada K7S 3G8

www.AsselinGroup.com

Copyright © 2014 Barb Asselin
First Printed June 6, 2014

All Rights reserved. No part of this book may be reproduced or used in any way or form or by any means whether electronic or mechanical, this means that you cannot record or photocopy any material ideas or text or graphics that are provided in this book.

My Running Log Book
My Personal Journal for Running Success

Table of Contents

Table of Contents 3

Introduction 5

Training Log 9

Conclusion 61

Enjoy this book? 62

INTRODUCTION

Congratulations! You have made the first step towards your running success. Whether you are a first-time runner who needs motivation to get off the couch, or if you are a veteran marathoner, this journal will help you succeed.

Inside, you will find the following sections for each week of training:

- **Week** – indicate the month and week of training
- **Date** – log each day of exercise on a separate line
- **Distance** – log how far you ran or walked
- **Time** – log how long it took to complete your distance
- **Average pace** – calculate your average pace in either miles or kilometers
- **Heart rate** – if you have a heart rate monitor, or monitor your heart rate manually, record it here
- **Route** – indicate the route you took during your run
- **Notes** – a spot for you to note the weather, or any other items of interest such as a busy day, special plans, injuries, etc.
- **Weekly distance** – record your total mileage for the week
- **Year-to-date distance** – record your total mileage to date for the year
- **Weight** – indicate your weight at the beginning of end of the week, and
- **Cross training** – indicate whether or not you incorporated any cross training activities into your exercise plan this week.

If you are a beginning runner, make sure you are prepared for success:

- Have you checked with a physician before starting a new exercise plan?
- Do you have the necessary equipment for running, notably proper running shoes? There is nothing worse than sore feet or shin splints, which are a definite possibility without proper running shoes.
- Are you realistic about your ability? If you are just starting out, it is not realistic to run 5km, but it is realistic to walk 2-3km with a few minutes of running when you can.
- Do you have a running buddy? Often, being accountable to someone can make the difference between failure and success.
- Have you planned an appropriate healthy eating plan while you are training? Eating healthy foods will improve your performance while exercising. Alternatively, going out for a run after eating a hamburger and fries will be very difficult.
- Do you have a plan of attack? If you are just starting out, here is a 10-week example training program to get you to run 3km straight (note that there are workout plans for three days each week – feel free to do more if you can):

Week 1

Day 1: Walk 3km at your own pace – time yourself

Day 2: Walk 3km at a faster pace than before

Day 3: Run 1 minute, walk 3 minutes for the whole 3km

Week 2

>Day 1: Run 1 minute, walk 3 minutes

>Day 2: Run 1 minute, walk 3 minutes

>Day 3: Run 1 minute, walk 2 minutes

Week 3

>Day 1: Run 1 minute, walk 2 minutes

>Day 2: Run 1 minute, walk 2 minutes

>Day 3: Run 1 minute, walk 1 minute

Week 4

>Day 1: Run 1 minute, walk 1 minute

>Day 2: Run 1 minute, walk 1 minute

>Day 3: Run 2 minutes, walk 1 minute

Week 5

>Day 1: Run 2 minutes, walk 1 minute

>Day 2: Run 3 minutes, walk 1 minute

>Day 3: Run 3 minutes, walk 1 minute

Week 6

>Day 1: Run 4 minutes, walk 1 minute

>Day 2: Run 4 minutes, walk 1 minute

Day 3: Run 5 minutes, walk 1 minute

Week 7

Day 1: Run 5 minutes, walk 1 minute

Day 2: Run 6 minutes, walk 1 minute

Day 3: Run 6 minutes, walk 1 minute

Week 8

Day 1: Run 7 minutes, walk 1 minute

Day 2: Run 7 minutes, walk 1 minute

Day 3: Run 8 minutes, walk 1 minute

Week 9

Day 1: Run 8 minutes, walk 1 minute

Day 2: Run 9 minutes, walk 1 minute

Day 3: Run 9 minutes, walk 1 minute

Week 10

Day 1: Run 10 minutes, walk 1 minute

Day 2: Run 10 minutes, walk 1 minute

Day 3: Run 3km! Congrats!

There are enough log pages in this book for a full year or 52 weeks of running.

Have fun and happy running!

My Running Log Book

TRAINING LOG

Week of: _____

Date	Distance	Time	Avg. Pace	H/R	Route	Notes

Weekly/Year to Date Stats:

Weekly Distance	
YTD Distance	
Weight	
Cross Training	

My Running Log Book

Week of: _____

Date	Distance	Time	Avg. Pace	H/R	Route	Notes

Weekly/Year to Date Stats:

Weekly Distance	
YTD Distance	
Weight	
Cross Training	

Weekly Notes:

_____

_____

_____

My Running Log Book

Week of: _____

Date	Distance	Time	Avg. Pace	H/R	Route	Notes

Weekly/Year to Date Stats:

Weekly Distance	
YTD Distance	
Weight	
Cross Training	

Weekly Notes:
_____
_____
_____

My Running Log Book

Week of: _____

Date	Distance	Time	Avg. Pace	H/R	Route	Notes

Weekly/Year to Date Stats:

Weekly Distance	
YTD Distance	
Weight	
Cross Training	

Weekly Notes:

_____

_____

_____

My Running Log Book

Week of: _____

Date	Distance	Time	Avg. Pace	H/R	Route	Notes

Weekly/Year to Date Stats:

Weekly Distance	
YTD Distance	
Weight	
Cross Training	

Weekly Notes:

_____
_____
_____

Week of: _____

Date	Distance	Time	Avg. Pace	H/R	Route	Notes

Weekly/Year to Date Stats:

Weekly Distance	
YTD Distance	
Weight	
Cross Training	

Weekly Notes:

_____

_____

_____

My Running Log Book

Week of: _____

Date	Distance	Time	Avg. Pace	H/R	Route	Notes

Weekly/Year to Date Stats:

Weekly Distance	
YTD Distance	
Weight	
Cross Training	

Weekly Notes:

_____

_____

_____

My Running Log Book

Week of: _____

Date	Distance	Time	Avg. Pace	H/R	Route	Notes

Weekly/Year to Date Stats:

Weekly Distance	
YTD Distance	
Weight	
Cross Training	

Weekly Notes:

_____

_____

_____

My Running Log Book

Week of: _____

Date	Distance	Time	Avg. Pace	H/R	Route	Notes

Weekly/Year to Date Stats:

Weekly Distance	
YTD Distance	
Weight	
Cross Training	

Weekly Notes:

_____

_____

_____

My Running Log Book

Week of: _____

Date	Distance	Time	Avg. Pace	H/R	Route	Notes

Weekly/Year to Date Stats:

Weekly Distance	
YTD Distance	
Weight	
Cross Training	

Weekly Notes:

_____

_____

_____

My Running Log Book

Week of: _____

Date	Distance	Time	Avg. Pace	H/R	Route	Notes

Weekly/Year to Date Stats:

Weekly Distance	
YTD Distance	
Weight	
Cross Training	

Weekly Notes:

_____
_____
_____

Week of: _____

Date	Distance	Time	Avg. Pace	H/R	Route	Notes

Weekly/Year to Date Stats:

Weekly Distance	
YTD Distance	
Weight	
Cross Training	

Weekly Notes:

_____

_____

_____

My Running Log Book

Week of: _____

Date	Distance	Time	Avg. Pace	H/R	Route	Notes

Weekly/Year to Date Stats:

Weekly Distance	
YTD Distance	
Weight	
Cross Training	

Weekly Notes:

_____

_____

_____

Week of: _____

Date	Distance	Time	Avg. Pace	H/R	Route	Notes

Weekly/Year to Date Stats:

Weekly Distance	
YTD Distance	
Weight	
Cross Training	

Weekly Notes:

_____
_____
_____

My Running Log Book

Week of: _____

Date	Distance	Time	Avg. Pace	H/R	Route	Notes

Weekly/Year to Date Stats:

Weekly Distance	
YTD Distance	
Weight	
Cross Training	

Weekly Notes:

_____

_____

_____

Week of: _____

Date	Distance	Time	Avg. Pace	H/R	Route	Notes

Weekly/Year to Date Stats:

Weekly Distance	
YTD Distance	
Weight	
Cross Training	

Weekly Notes:

_____
_____
_____

My Running Log Book

Week of: _____

Date	Distance	Time	Avg. Pace	H/R	Route	Notes

Weekly/Year to Date Stats:

Weekly Distance	
YTD Distance	
Weight	
Cross Training	

Weekly Notes:

_____

_____

_____

My Running Log Book

Week of: _____

Date	Distance	Time	Avg. Pace	H/R	Route	Notes

Weekly/Year to Date Stats:

Weekly Distance	
YTD Distance	
Weight	
Cross Training	

Weekly Notes:

_____

_____

_____

My Running Log Book

Week of: _____

Date	Distance	Time	Avg. Pace	H/R	Route	Notes

Weekly/Year to Date Stats:

Weekly Distance	
YTD Distance	
Weight	
Cross Training	

Weekly Notes:

_____
_____
_____

Week of: _____

Date	Distance	Time	Avg. Pace	H/R	Route	Notes

Weekly/Year to Date Stats:

Weekly Distance	
YTD Distance	
Weight	
Cross Training	

Weekly Notes:

_____

_____

_____

My Running Log Book

Week of: _____

Date	Distance	Time	Avg. Pace	H/R	Route	Notes

Weekly/Year to Date Stats:

Weekly Distance	
YTD Distance	
Weight	
Cross Training	

Weekly Notes:

_____

_____

_____

My Running Log Book

Week of: _____

Date	Distance	Time	Avg. Pace	H/R	Route	Notes

Weekly/Year to Date Stats:

Weekly Distance	
YTD Distance	
Weight	
Cross Training	

Weekly Notes:

_____

_____

_____

My Running Log Book

Week of: _____

Date	Distance	Time	Avg. Pace	H/R	Route	Notes

Weekly/Year to Date Stats:

Weekly Distance	
YTD Distance	
Weight	
Cross Training	

Weekly Notes:

_____

_____

_____

Week of: _____

Date	Distance	Time	Avg. Pace	H/R	Route	Notes

Weekly/Year to Date Stats:

Weekly Distance	
YTD Distance	
Weight	
Cross Training	

Weekly Notes:

_____
_____
_____

My Running Log Book

Week of: _____

Date	Distance	Time	Avg. Pace	H/R	Route	Notes

Weekly/Year to Date Stats:

Weekly Distance	
YTD Distance	
Weight	
Cross Training	

Weekly Notes:
_____
_____
_____

Week of: _____

Date	Distance	Time	Avg. Pace	H/R	Route	Notes

Weekly/Year to Date Stats:

Weekly Distance	
YTD Distance	
Weight	
Cross Training	

Weekly Notes:

_____
_____
_____

My Running Log Book

Week of: _____

Date	Distance	Time	Avg. Pace	H/R	Route	Notes

Weekly/Year to Date Stats:

Weekly Distance	
YTD Distance	
Weight	
Cross Training	

Weekly Notes:

_____

_____

_____

Week of: _____

Date	Distance	Time	Avg. Pace	H/R	Route	Notes

Weekly/Year to Date Stats:

Weekly Distance	
YTD Distance	
Weight	
Cross Training	

Weekly Notes:

_____

_____

_____

My Running Log Book

Week of: _____

Date	Distance	Time	Avg. Pace	H/R	Route	Notes

Weekly/Year to Date Stats:

Weekly Distance	
YTD Distance	
Weight	
Cross Training	

Weekly Notes:
_____
_____
_____

Week of: _____

Date	Distance	Time	Avg. Pace	H/R	Route	Notes

Weekly/Year to Date Stats:

Weekly Distance	
YTD Distance	
Weight	
Cross Training	

Weekly Notes:

_____

_____

_____

My Running Log Book

Week of: _____

Date	Distance	Time	Avg. Pace	H/R	Route	Notes

Weekly/Year to Date Stats:

Weekly Distance	
YTD Distance	
Weight	
Cross Training	

Weekly Notes:
_____
_____
_____

Week of: _____

Date	Distance	Time	Avg. Pace	H/R	Route	Notes

Weekly/Year to Date Stats:

Weekly Distance	
YTD Distance	
Weight	
Cross Training	

Weekly Notes:

_____
_____
_____

My Running Log Book

Week of: _____

Date	Distance	Time	Avg. Pace	H/R	Route	Notes

Weekly/Year to Date Stats:

Weekly Distance	
YTD Distance	
Weight	
Cross Training	

Weekly Notes:

_____

_____

_____

Week of: _____

Date	Distance	Time	Avg. Pace	H/R	Route	Notes

Weekly/Year to Date Stats:

Weekly Distance	
YTD Distance	
Weight	
Cross Training	

Weekly Notes:

_____
_____
_____

My Running Log Book

Week of: _____

Date	Distance	Time	Avg. Pace	H/R	Route	Notes

Weekly/Year to Date Stats:

Weekly Distance	
YTD Distance	
Weight	
Cross Training	

Weekly Notes:
_____
_____
_____

Week of: _____

Date	Distance	Time	Avg. Pace	H/R	Route	Notes

Weekly/Year to Date Stats:

Weekly Distance	
YTD Distance	
Weight	
Cross Training	

Weekly Notes:

_____
_____
_____

My Running Log Book

Week of: _____

Date	Distance	Time	Avg. Pace	H/R	Route	Notes

Weekly/Year to Date Stats:

Weekly Distance	
YTD Distance	
Weight	
Cross Training	

Weekly Notes:

_____

_____

_____

Week of: _____

Date	Distance	Time	Avg. Pace	H/R	Route	Notes

Weekly/Year to Date Stats:

Weekly Distance	
YTD Distance	
Weight	
Cross Training	

Weekly Notes:

_____

_____

_____

My Running Log Book

Week of: _____

Date	Distance	Time	Avg. Pace	H/R	Route	Notes

Weekly/Year to Date Stats:

Weekly Distance	
YTD Distance	
Weight	
Cross Training	

Weekly Notes:

_____
_____
_____

Week of: _____

Date	Distance	Time	Avg. Pace	H/R	Route	Notes

Weekly/Year to Date Stats:

Weekly Distance	
YTD Distance	
Weight	
Cross Training	

Weekly Notes:
_____
_____
_____

My Running Log Book

Week of: _____

Date	Distance	Time	Avg. Pace	H/R	Route	Notes

Weekly/Year to Date Stats:

Weekly Distance	
YTD Distance	
Weight	
Cross Training	

Weekly Notes:

_____
_____
_____

My Running Log Book

Week of: _____

Date	Distance	Time	Avg. Pace	H/R	Route	Notes

Weekly/Year to Date Stats:

Weekly Distance	
YTD Distance	
Weight	
Cross Training	

Weekly Notes:

_____

_____

_____

My Running Log Book

Week of: _____

Date	Distance	Time	Avg. Pace	H/R	Route	Notes

Weekly/Year to Date Stats:

Weekly Distance	
YTD Distance	
Weight	
Cross Training	

Weekly Notes:
_____
_____
_____

Week of: _____

Date	Distance	Time	Avg. Pace	H/R	Route	Notes

Weekly/Year to Date Stats:

Weekly Distance	
YTD Distance	
Weight	
Cross Training	

Weekly Notes:
_____
_____
_____

My Running Log Book

Week of: _____

Date	Distance	Time	Avg. Pace	H/R	Route	Notes

Weekly/Year to Date Stats:

Weekly Distance	
YTD Distance	
Weight	
Cross Training	

Weekly Notes:
_____
_____
_____

Week of: _____

Date	Distance	Time	Avg. Pace	H/R	Route	Notes

Weekly/Year to Date Stats:

Weekly Distance	
YTD Distance	
Weight	
Cross Training	

Weekly Notes:

_____
_____
_____

My Running Log Book

Week of: _____

Date	Distance	Time	Avg. Pace	H/R	Route	Notes

Weekly/Year to Date Stats:

Weekly Distance	
YTD Distance	
Weight	
Cross Training	

Weekly Notes:

_____

_____

_____

Week of: _____

Date	Distance	Time	Avg. Pace	H/R	Route	Notes

Weekly/Year to Date Stats:

Weekly Distance	
YTD Distance	
Weight	
Cross Training	

Weekly Notes:

_____

_____

_____

My Running Log Book

Week of: _____

Date	Distance	Time	Avg. Pace	H/R	Route	Notes

Weekly/Year to Date Stats:

Weekly Distance	
YTD Distance	
Weight	
Cross Training	

Weekly Notes:

_____
_____
_____

Week of: _____

Date	Distance	Time	Avg. Pace	H/R	Route	Notes

Weekly/Year to Date Stats:

Weekly Distance	
YTD Distance	
Weight	
Cross Training	

Weekly Notes:

_____

_____

_____

My Running Log Book

Week of: _____

Date	Distance	Time	Avg. Pace	H/R	Route	Notes

Weekly/Year to Date Stats:

Weekly Distance	
YTD Distance	
Weight	
Cross Training	

Weekly Notes:
_____
_____
_____

Week of: _____

Date	Distance	Time	Avg. Pace	H/R	Route	Notes

Weekly/Year to Date Stats:

Weekly Distance	
YTD Distance	
Weight	
Cross Training	

Weekly Notes:

_____
_____
_____

Conclusion

Well, how did your training go? Did you reach your goal to get off the couch and start running? Or, did you run your first half-marathon? Whatever your goals were at the outset, I hope you made progress towards them.

Whenever I take a break from running, I always go back to the 10 week starter plan and get to my 3km per day. Then, I focus on something bigger. My favorite thing to do is to sign up for a local 5km run with my husband and children. There is something about signing up for an event that is motivating. The clock is ticking and the race will arrive whether I am ready or not, so that motivates me to train for it. It is also a great way to engage my family in a daily exercise routine.

If you have already completed a few 5km, why not try a longer distance? Nothing is beyond your reach if you train properly. If running a marathon is on your bucket list, then find one that is a good distance away and start training! Or, find a half-marathon and complete that first. Then, you will have a better idea of what it will take to complete a full marathon.

Good luck and happy running!

ENJOY THIS BOOK?

You've made it all the way to the end of our book. I'm so glad you enjoyed it enough to get all the way through! If you liked the book, would you be open to leaving it a 4 or 5 star review? You see when people like you are able to give self-published authors a review, it helps us out in a big way. You can leave a review for this book at the Amazon page for this book.

It'd really mean a lot to me.

Thank you.

Barb Asselin

Made in the USA
Middletown, DE
06 May 2017